ALASKA

MALLARD
PRESS

Photography
FPG
Odyssey Publishing Ltd

Photo Editor
Annette Lerner

MALLARD PRESS

An imprint of BDD Promotional
Book Company Inc.,
666 Fifth Avenue, New York,
NY 10103

Mallard Press and its
accompanying design and logo
are trademarks of BDD
Promotional Book Company, Inc.

Color separations by Advance
Laser Graphic Arts, Hong Kong.

Printed and bound
in Hong Kong.

ISBN 0-7924-5485-5

*Previous pages: the Alaska
Range. Right: musher and dog
team on Iditarod Trail near Nome.*

Andrew Johnson is usually remembered as the only American President who was impeached. It doesn't matter that he was acquitted. The same Congress that couldn't get rid of him became single-minded about besmirching his name, and in the process the name of Alaska was tarred with the same brush.

When Johnson's Secretary of State, William H. Seward, negotiated the purchase of Alaska from the Russians for $7.2 million in 1867, he left paying the bill up to Congress. It was a golden opportunity to make the President look like a deadbeat, and they bottled up the request in the appropriations committee. More than a year went by before Tsar Alexander II got his money and, during that year, Alaska was the centerpiece of one of the nastiest debates Washington had ever seen.

In fact, many Americans still believe some of the slurs that appeared in the record of the 40th Congress, which characterized the territory as cold, barren and unfit for human habitation. Most people would agree that it was worth two cents an acre, more or less what was paid for the vastness of Alaska, but in the halls of Congress it was denounced as highway robbery.

When the shouting was over Congress tried to forget about the whole thing. They passed a law setting import duties, turned over seal hunting rights to a politically well-connected company and ordered troops sent there to keep the natives cool. But for the duration of the next eight Congresses and the terms of four presidents, the name Alaska was a dirty word in Washington.

During that time there were no laws in the Territory. It wasn't possible to buy or sell property, to get married or divorced, to collect an inheritance. An army force was stationed there to keep order, but when the Indians began to make trouble in Idaho, the soldiers were shipped out and the job turned over to the customs collector, the only government official on the scene. His men weren't too enthusiastic about their new duties, and they petitioned the President to send a warship to help. He was slow to answer, but when the ship finally arrived, its captain had orders to take over the government until Congress could get around to setting up a new one. It took them five more years, during which time all of Alaska was governed by the captain of a ship which was anchored off the coast.

When Congress finally did get its act together, seventeen long years had passed since Seward had made the original deal. And what they came up with after all that time was a carbon copy of the laws in effect in Oregon. As far as the lawmakers were concerned this made perfect sense. Oregon was out there somewhere in the Northwest and so was Alaska. How different could they be?

Attitudes began to change when gold was discovered in the Klondike and prospectors noticed that there was just as much across the border in Alaska. In the first ten years of the twentieth century, Alaska's population more than doubled. No Alaskan has ever been accused of being docile, but the newcomers were more vocal than the people who had been agitating all those years for more recognition. They began a massive letter-writing campaign and, in 1912, Congress finally got the message. They decided there were differences between Alaska and Oregon and not the least of them was that Oregonians had their own representatives in Congress and Alaskans didn't.

Still, it took a long debate for them to do anything about it. What finally pushed them over in the direction of creating a territorial government that could deal with Alaskan problems was a matter of money. Pencil pushers among them figured that after the original $7.2 million it had cost them to buy, the Federal Government had spent just $35 million on Alaska in forty-five years. In the same period, the territory had returned $450 million to the treasury.

It made sense, even to the dullards among them, that with a little control the bottom line could be enhanced considerably. But even with a territorial government in place, they went right on treating Alaska as a poor relative.

World War II changed all that. Airports and military bases brought in new people and they liked Alaska well enough to want to stay. Moreover, they loved it enough to want it to become a state. Actually, Congress had been debating that question since 1916. Finally on January 3, 1959, it became the 49th state of the United States. The long debate was over at last.

Right: the bronze plaque at Isabel Pass on the Richardson Highway, commemorating General Wilds P. Richardson, the first president of the Alaskan Road Commission. Below: the snow-capped peak of Mount Kimball towers above the Alaska Range, rising to a height of 10,000 feet. Facing page: a sailboat on Alaska's Inside Passage flanked by Tongass National Forest. The 1,000-mile-long, island-studded waterway stretches from lower British Columbia in Canada to the top of southeastern Alaska.

Facing page: the 1914,
plantation-style Governor's
Mansion in the State Capital,
Juneau. Juneau today is a far cry
from the wilderness that Joe
Juneau and Dick Harris
encountered in 1880 when they
were searching for gold. Despite
the rich seam they unearthed,
Juneau died so poor that a public
collection was required to raise
the money to send his body home
to the city he co-founded. Above:
a replica log cabin church in the
Juneau Visitor Center, built in
1980 for the city's centennial
celebrations. Right: the Universe
and Juneau City seen from
Gastineau Channel.

Below: a ski lift in the Eaglescrest Ski Area, twelve miles from Juneau, on Douglas Island. Right: floatplanes near Juneau. Such 'planes are a popular means of travel, for despite being on the mainland, Juneau is only accessible by air or sea – beyond the towering mountains surrounding the city lies the 4,000-square-mile Juneau Icefield.

Left: the rugged coast of Saint Paul, one of the Pribilof Islands, and (facing page) an Inuit boy in a village on Anaktuvuk Pass. The Pribilof Islands, Saint Paul and Saint George, are home to a multitude of seabirds, as well as being home to the world's largest Aleut community.

Right: Steller sea lions. Below: Adam's Inlet, in Glacier Bay National Park (facing page). When Captain George Vancouver visited the area in 1786, the entrance to Glacier Bay was completely choked with ice. However, when naturalist John Muir visited later, in 1879, the ice had retreated thirty-two miles, and a further twenty-four miles had vanished by 1916 – the fastest recorded glacial retreat. Glacier Bay National Park covers 3.3 million scenic acres in Alaska's Panhandle.

These pages: the wildlife of Alaska, and (above) the island of Saint Paul, one of the Pribilof Islands. In the words of Henry Gannett: "one of the chief assets of Alaska, if not the greatest, is the scenery. There are glaciers, mountains, and fjords elsewhere but nowhere on earth in such abundance and magnificence. For one Yosemite Alaska has a hundred. The mountains and glaciers of the Cascade Range are duplicated a thousand fold in Alaska, its grandeur more valuable than gold, fish, or timber, for it will never be exhausted."

The small boat harbor at Valdez. Boats are often more useful to Alaskans than cars, as roads are often rudimentary or nonexistent, while most places are accessible by sea or river.

Left: a Yupik woman collecting wild celery on Nunivak Island. These days Nunivak is the only island in the Bering Sea that still boasts wild reindeer. Below: the Yukon River Valley near Circle. Circle was so named by the prospectors who founded it because they mistakenly thought they were within the Arctic Circle. Facing page: sunset over Mineral Creek, near Valdez. Mineral Creek flows directly from a glacier of the same name to the north of Valdez.

Valdez under snow. In December and January it is only light from mid-morning to mid-afternoon, so all business has to be done largely in darkness and often in adverse weather conditions.

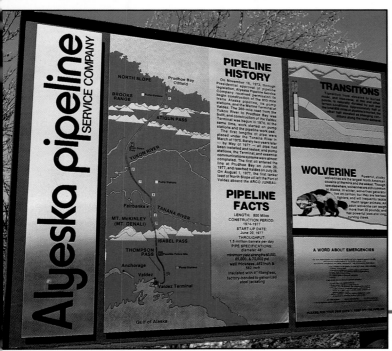

Above and left: the Trans-Alaska Pipeline. This amazing feat of engineering zig-zags its way 800 miles across Alaska, from Pudhoe Bay, within the Arctic Circle, to Valdez on the Gulf of Alaska. It was completed in 1977, having taken just two years to construct. Some sections are held above ground to prevent heat from the pipe thawing the permafrost and, consequently, eroding the tundra. The zig-zag form gives it greater flexibility to expand and contract. Far left: a satellite tracking station run by NASA at Gilmore Creek.

Left: Sitka Harbor. Aleksander Baranov of the Russian American Company established a Russian outpost here in 1799 to exploit the area's natural abundance of fur seals and sea otters. The outpost also traded in ice and fish, and was a major stopping-off port for merchant ships en route to Asia. However, the natural supplies of fish and fur were soon depleted and, by 1867, when America bought Alaska from Russia, Sitka's economy was failing. The sale of Alaska was completed in Sitka in what is now the Castle Hill Historic Site. Below: hopeful prospectors panning for gold in the waters around Fairbanks. Facing page: thaw in Denali National Park and Preserve.

Mount McKinley, towering out of the Alaska Range in Denali National Park and Preserve. This 20,320-foot peak is known as Denali, "The Great One."

Above: the Ruth Glacier beside Mount McKinley, flowing down the Alaska Range of mountains through Denali National Park and Preserve (these pages). Right: Mount McKinley in late September, seen from Wonder Lake. The north peak of Mount McKinley was first scaled by two miners, Billy Taylor and Pete Anderson, in 1910. This was their first-ever climb, and it was probably their inexperience that led them to believe they had scaled the summit rather than the lower north peak.

Most of Alaska's roads converge in Anchorage (left and facing page top), as do many of the world's flight paths, leading the city to refer to itself as the "air crossroads of the world" – Anchorage Airport is famous as the place where President Ronald Reagan had a meeting with Pope John Paul II. Anchorage is Alaska's largest and most central city. Facing page bottom: Highway One, known as Glenn Highway, south of Anchorage.

The Iditarod Trail Sled Dog Race (facing page) covers 1,049 miles between Anchorage and Nome. The race, billed as "The Last Great Race on Earth," commemorates an actual race for life in 1925 when mushers rushed diphtheria serum from Nenana to Nome to staunch an epidemic there in 1925. There was no other way to get the vital medicine over the snow-bound wilderness, and stout-hearted dogs and mushers managed a trip that normally took more than a month in a few days. The race is not non-stop, however: dogs are mushed as far as Eagle River and then loaded into trucks and taken to Knik for a second start. Right: a husky, and (below) Nikolai International Airport, on the Iditarod Trail to Nome.

Facing page: (top) bush pilots' skiplanes on Iditarod Lake, a vital link for Alaskans with the outside world, and (bottom) a boat at Point Barrow. Right: Copper River, running through the Kenai Mountains on the Kenai Peninsula and traversing the border of Wrangell-Saint Elias National Park under a glorious sky. The sheer beauty of Alaska is something that no visitor can fully anticipate. Sunsets are routinely breathtaking.

Below: the catch of the day in Homer, on Kachemak Bay. Homer subsists on halibut fishing, but the variety of sea life to be found off Homer is rich and plentiful. Right: Seward Harbor. Seward was founded in 1903, and was for many years Alaska's leading port, eventually being overtaken in prominence by Anchorage. Seward has only recently recovered from the devastation it sustained during the 1964 earthquake.

Facing page: a disused gold
dredger near Fairbanks. It was
gold that lured settlers to
Fairbanks and the Interior, and
the town sprang up almost
accidentally in 1901 when E.T.
Barnette and his family tried to set
up a trade post on the Tanana
River to rival Chicago. They didn't
reach their original site since the
river was unnavigable, so they set
up shop on the Chena.
Subsequent gold strikes in the
region led to an influx of
prospectors and the birth of the
city. Above: a Russian chapel at
Eklutna. Left: a colorful Indian
graveyard.

Right: the telecommunications dish on the winter-bound shore of Nome (below), on the Bering Sea. Like many other settlements in Alaska, Nome was originally a gold-boom town. Over 22,000 people rushed there after a strike was made on the beach. Its present-day population is just under 3,500, and it is still possible to pan for gold on the beach.

Left: the ice flow on Turnagain Arm, the thin finger of Cook Inlet that separates the peninsula from the Anchorage Bowl, and (above) Tongass National Forest. Facing page: a young boy walking across mudflats in Cordova. Cordova is a railroad town and has been since April 1, 1906, when Michael J. Heney arrived there with a shipload of equipment and men in his endeavor to construct the Copper River and Northwestern Railway. He had to contend with temperatures below -50°C, and winds that knocked boxcars off their tracks. Overleaf: a rainbow arches over caribou in Denali National Park.